CHEMO-POET AND OTHER POEMS

also by Helene Davis
Nightblind

CHEMO-POET
AND OTHER POEMS

BY

HELENE DAVIS

ALICE JAMES BOOKS
CAMBRIDGE, MASSACHUSETTS
1989

Library of Congress Cataloging-in-Publication Data
I. Chemo-Poet
PS3554. A934634C44 1989
811' .54--dc 19   88-31560 CIP

ISBN 0-914086-87-1

Sculpture on cover by Paul Gray.
Cover design, illustration, and book design by Anna M. Pulaski.
Typeset by The Writer's Center, Bethesda, Maryland.
Printed by Wickersham Press, Lancaster, Pennsylvania.

Alice James Books are published by the Alice James Publishing
Cooperative, Inc.

Alice James Books
33 Richdale Avenue
Cambridge, MA 02140

ACKNOWLEDGMENTS

I would like to thank the editors of the following publications, in which versions of these poems originally appeared:

Nightblind Pourboire Press — The Distances Between Us, I Will Not Change My Name, I'm Nobody's Dream Girl, Only My Own, The Cold Bed, Women Do Not Ripen Early, Life Model, Park Drive Paranoia

Prairie Schooner — Chemo-Poet, The Generic Oncologist, My World, I Dream, Healing By Computer, The Prince, I Visit the Prosthesis Lady

Southern Poetry Review — The Cold Bed

The Black Warrior Review — Peeping Tom, The Net, The Occupant, Chair and Bench, Park Drive Paranoia, The Burning Window: Variations on a Theme, The Red Shoes, Ira

Ploughshares — The Interior, The Slide, Farmers, Weather—Chance of Snow

The Blacksmith Anthology 11 Women Do Not Ripen Early

The poems appearing in *The Black Warrior Review* won the Black Warrior Literary Competition for 1977.

The publication of this book was made possible with support from the Massachusetts Council on the Arts and Humanities, a state agency whose funds are recommended by the Governor and appropriated by the State Legislature, and from the National Endowment for the Arts, Washington, D.C.

For Paul Gray and Martha Collins

CONTENTS

CHEMO-POET

THE BLUES

AVOIDING HEAD-ON COLLISIONS

LAUGHING IN CHINESE

We're riding the subway together and only you
know where we're going. I trust you completely
but everyone here is in on a secret. They're jabbering
and laughing in Chinese. I've been away for a long
time, but they remember how I let everything die
in my house, how I neglected the cat, let strangers bury it.
How the plants withered in the filthy rooms, how my days
cracked apart like dice. How nothing matched.

You tell me we'll have dinner together, drinks.
When I drink, I can raise the dead. You remember
when I burned down your house, married your lover?
You point to the woman at my side in the silk dress
who is laughing so hard tears run over her hands.
You catch on, cover your mouth with lace.

I know my shoes don't match and I'm put together
with safety pins and some old woman's underthings.
I have a picture of a woman inside a tornado calling
for help. I hold it to my breast as if it were
the child I left behind in one of the countries I visited.
You are my friend. I have never forgotten you.
When I tell you that I love you, you lead me to the exit
as if I were blind.

THE DISTANCES BETWEEN US

The available city of light
is not the promised land.
It is a catechism of shapes
and neon signs saying
walk in a straight line.

It is the ready genius of snowflakes
in a dark room, the woman
who is the Snow Queen. All her seasons
are winter. She walks through the park
with a whip, urging old men into gutters,
begging lovers to part.

The frost on the pumpkin is sea green
and glows in the dark, the fate
of the princess is not for us to decide.

My darling, the distances between us
are the moon's last thought,
the child we never had,
the lightbulb that is God,
blinking on and off.

WEATHER — CHANCE OF SNOW

You tell me you will be my true
false bottom to my suitcase,
more luggage than anyone can carry.

The snow falls easily at first, as if
it were meant to be, as if
it had no choice,
then harder, as if it were leaving home.

At home we watch the snow
through windows of a haunted house, or watch
for a chance of snow, a chance to huddle together,
easily at first, as if it were meant to be,

like coming home with a full suitcase
after a good trip, happy to find your true
false-hearted lover waiting, hands
filled with early snow,

snow on the mantlepiece, snow
on the bed where once you slept,
easily as if it were meant.

I WILL NOT CHANGE MY NAME

to fit your hand. Already
I'm bigger than the blanket
that covers you, though you make
a big noise in my house, a heyday
for my nightmares.

Uneasy among my animals
you move through my house
like a guest, a nonbeliever.
A beggar at the backdoor once,
now head of the table.
A Marlboro man with a briefcase,
a key to my door.

WASHING THE NUDE

Aristide Maillol's Nude, "Nymph"
The Hirshhorn Sculpture Garden
Washington, D.C.

It's just a job, he thinks.
Outdoor sculpture must be preserved
at any cost: mild soap, oils, paint.
But this one is different, he knows.
He is wearing jeans, a red bandanna.
Suddenly he is way back when
he had never before touched a woman
with fondness. There would be a time
for that. In time he would recognize
a woman who asked nothing of him
but to remain the faithful record
of someone's dream. Never to grow old,
never to ask questions.

If she has a name, he has not yet
searched for it. He is competent. He warms
her tight buttocks. Her nipples melt
into his restoring hands. All in a day's work.
She knows he will not get roped in.
He chose his weather: perfect. His woman:
unending. Yet she knows what it means
to touch and not be moved, to grow
around someone's body, then walk away
leaving only his image timeless, intact.

YOU ARE AIRBORNE

I am the only one left at the airport,
stuck in my shoes, the ones that fit.
Winter gloves and a loose coat.
Outside, others say goodby as if
they mean it. Red fingernails on glass.
Children cry and want to go home.
In this dream the heat buzzes like insects.

My grandfather keeps watch. He is everything
I ever wanted in a grandfather: burly and
dramatic, nose like a fist in his dark face.
Exits and entrances in his voice, stories
that once echoed through the ghetto streets.

He is determined to be here, to witness
our separation. My old *Zayde,* the gypsy.
He is trying to tell me something but I hear you
leaving me, your slow, bumbling talk, talk, talk.

You are airborne. The sky hangs in shreds,
grey as suitcases piled up like tombstones.
Then—a razor of light. You, going somewhere
like Montana, or Kentucky.

There is always a clock in dreams,
but my grandfather's face points east,
and we take the wineglasses and the Bible
which says *Whither thou goest* out of the cabinet
and start a prayer neither of us remembers.

My grandfather takes his time, knows
he doesn't belong in this dream. He remembers
how he hung on forever after he died,
how he wore out his welcome.

IRA

Do what you wish. The old man covers
his head and fasts from sundown
to sundown, and doesn't care
if *you* observe the holidays, even
if your backgrounds are similar. He watches
the days fall away like the doors of an old
house, the neighborhood deteriorate.

He is not the man your grandmother
married, or the uncle whose lap
you sat on, begging for a story.
You wouldn't want to know him. Now,
his wife is dead, his children pick
their way through stone houses
in Miami.

The *mezuzah* over your doorway
means nothing to him either. He is
blind to the traditions you continue
without thought. The waitress in the deli
snickers behind his back, the crumbs
on his coat, his hands carefully folded,
the tattooed numbers on his wrist,
the repetitions of the old prayers.

I'M NOBODY'S DREAM GIRL,
ONLY MY OWN

Turned inside out
or through a keyhole,
I'm just like any other woman
only I have a child every day,

and the snag-toothed dog
in the kitchen
will kill any thief
who tries to get in.

Yesterday, my son played Adam
in a trick of light,
spreading his hands for Eve,
and today I crouch by the bed
hoping Ruth will come out
well again.

Only in dreams the truth
thunders like Job at God,
and I awaken ashamed in the morning
with another child on the way,
fatherless as I am.

THE COLD BED

The rip in my fur coat
looks like the flap wound
on a scalp after surgery.
And what would they have taken out,
pulling memories like corks,
catching anger in ceramic bowls?

In the cold bed
the books I read
heat areas I refuse to touch.
I want one cold place
to freeze hell over.

And what of the dreams
that arrange themselves in a circle
of straight-backed chairs? With nothing soft
to sit on, they ache and grin,
folding their hands like nuns.
They touch ever so softly
my belly, my black crotch.

Folding themselves over and over again,
they cry forget! forget!
Wear your fur coat through the streets
like an old woman, tell children lies.
Remember the child you killed, and the child
your mother sent to a convent
telling her she was bad, bad.

WOMEN DO NOT RIPEN EARLY

in Providence, Rhode Island. Every
progress they make is raked back
like autumn leaves, and their bodies
are suspended in time.

Burning at eighteen
they are sent into the world,
breasts plastered on bone,
a threat of blood. They carry
no images, no identification.

Lost perhaps in Boston, New York,
the midwest, they stand out
like missionaries, not
knowing the language, or
department store mannequins.

In dreams they climb
again and again
the hill where the Fleur de Lis building
waits like a temple,

and although they have parents, cousins
they wish to forget, they keep going
back to visit, all the time knowing
a door will lock behind them,
they will never get out.

FRIDAY THE THIRTEENTH

Only on days like today
do I fade into the skin of my cat.
It is cold in May and the rain
grows like a fist that won't stop.

Outside, cars scramble for home,
and I live on the cold in my house
with the unending bare walls, the pink-
tinted light and the telephone that howls
like the wind "Come in, come in."

There's the quick bite of friends' voices
and Friday the Thirteenth waiting outside,
all jowls and teeth and recurrent dreams
of split-level houses, unfurnished.

Friday the Thirteenth: the unopened door,
the spitting rat, the race nobody wins.
I warn myself not to make plans today,
not to reach for the brass ring.

Forgotten Russian aunts and great-grandmothers
uttered curses that took root and worked:
the lame arm, the dead child. Sons of rabbis
and witches made their way here to build dreams and magic,

but you'd never know by my ordinary house
with the bright quilt and the clean
window and the black mouthpiece
connecting, connecting to everyone out there.

PARK DRIVE PARANOIA

The people who whisper in the hallway
do not even live in your building.
It has come to that. A strange key turns
in your door in the numb hours
of the dawn, but you dream
of words to use against the enemy.

You're blinded by the roads the enemy
takes to find you, the sacred paths. Hallways
in dreams always glimmer, and you dream
perfectly. You wake and build
magnificent clocks which count the hours
like petals. You like being alone, turn

to memory. Your dead father will return
to frighten you. The lake, the storm, the enemies
of your childhood, time and size. Hours
move off, neglected. Now you are in a hallway
with tiled floors, and somehow the building
you live in is falling apart. You dream

of moving out, but when? In your dreams
of the museum across the park the sculpture turns
like a knife. Old men try to build
the frame of an impossible house. The enemy
knows you cannot take care of yourself. Hallways
lead to a chamber of an old house where hours

are eaten by people like you. You use the hours
you have to plan. And although you refuse to dream
of tomorrow you do not live today. Your hallway
has no doors, no windows. A snake turns
on your lawn, nibbles on words. The enemy
is stout as the grass and lives in the building

you built for yourself. The brick the building
is made of contains you and your hourly
watch. The perfect face of the enemy
is one you chose, fashioned out of dreams
that are favorites. We will help you, take turns
with the doctors and clerks in the hallway

and dream you into something alive, build
a hallway around you and the hours
you spend with the enemy. Waiting your turn.

PEEPING TOM

The phone rings in an empty house.
No no no it says. But Peeping Tom knows
you are there, and why you won't answer the telephone
except when *he* calls.

And his voice is irresistible. After all, he knows
your habits, your daily rituals. And although he is
not necessarily your best friend, he knows more
about you than your friends do, about what matters
in your life.

When he found you, alone in the nakedness you wore
like silk to comfort you, he called, he let you
know, until you covered your windows the way
Jews cover mirrors for the dead.

And you shut out the moon, which has a bad taste
for you now, and the daylight, until you didn't
know the hour, the weather. You took his phone calls
as punishment for discovering, perhaps, your body,
or for loving the arch moonlight when it would come.

You don't except Peeping Tom will move
to another neighborhood. He will appear in your
dreams in a top hat and a black umbrella.
You will wait for him in the darkness he created.

AVOIDING HEAD-ON COLLISIONS

You've lost your boarding pass.
This has happened so often, you've learned
to accept it, know you don't want to take
this particular trip. But your mother
redeems you, has enough money to cover
your expenses, a new ticket. Suddenly
you are on your way back home again:
the familiar locked door, the thief
in the kitchen making himself at home.

■

Between the street signs, the stone fences,
the borders, your favorite, your very best
child furnishes the rooms of his imagination
with sticks that burn, chairs that collapse.
His invisible companion disappears
into the woods, rubs flint together
until you burst in that special place
in your belly, and you can't thank
him enough, and you forget your child
who stumbles home in the dark.

■

You anticipate your death, make lists
of possessions you wish to leave behind,
erase a lot. Your friends whisper,
laugh at what you saved, so carefully
cherished: the ruined paintings, the lock
of red hair, even your jade necklace.
The Buddha, legs crossed, is grinning

at you and will not light the way. Somewhere
in boxes and cabinets the fruits you harvested
will darken and disappear.

PICTURES

THE NET

The door opens on a badminton
court where the invisible players
shimmer with perspiration in the sun
under the azure blue sky. Love
has nothing to do with it. The players
are graceful and obey the rules.

The battering sun is blinding but not
to you and me. We know who they really
are, although they do not wish to be
believed, and hide behind myths
they built into their courtship.

The space between their conversation
is flecked with blue. We question
why the lovers are playing on a hot
weekday, why they are not at home
making love, why they remain unseen
behind the squared-off reality of
the net, the aluminum quality of the air.

CHAIR AND BENCH

The chair and the bench are perfectly
suited to one another and fit
into each other like lovers. They are
intoxicated with the arbitrary way they met.

They curse the hands that touch them,
the bodies that fit clumsily into
their secret parts. The blue of the
chair is the sea to the bench, the sky
falling hard into winter. The chair is easy
to please, loves the gentle slope
of the bench, its grainy laugh.

They have been together for years,
have found a place where they are almost
never troubled. They are growing old
together, becoming a single shape
in the gathering shadows.

PICTURES

I find your pictures
compelling, as if
I'd crawled through anybody's
window. But where are the people?
We need people. That's how we know
who we are. Am I

asking the wrong questions? I
could paint people. Those pictures
where the eyes follow you? You know
those eyes. But think. If
I invited people
to my house, anybody

could steal my time, anybody
could enter my visions. I
leave them in the dark; people
need the dark, become pictures
in their own dreams. If
I painted them, they'd know

they were alive somewhere, know
they could keep coming back. Anybody
would intrude, thinking I'd created them. If
light falling on glass moves you, I
understand. Light makes pictures
you don't have to obey, but people

want more. They come back, hungry. People
live in artificial light, know
how to make their own. *But your pictures*
worship beauty, give anybody
the gift of new eyes, real skin. I
want to go inside your pictures. If

I went inside, would you see me? If
you went inside? No. Not even now. People
blind me. They ask too much. I
feel my eyes fail when I know
someone is in my rooms. Anybody!
Look at my pictures.

Look hard at my pictures. Recognize anybody
you know? Yourself, perhaps, in that chair? If
you see yourself, I haven't failed. I know people.

THE INTERIOR

The interior is ordinary,
although at times
the light falls like sand,
the furniture edges into itself
and the far corners of the room relax
like seascapes in the numb hours.

Everything changes when a man
enters the room, especially
for women. A woman who is there
is unable to leave although she is
uncomfortable and remembers other times
she was unable to leave a room
although she cannot tell us why.

Early contact with men
and interiors has of course
gathered corners of rooms together
for her, made a prison of her desires.

And although she cannot and does not
wish to communicate with the man
in the room, she is moved by his silence,
his not letting go.

LIFE MODEL

I am nude and faceless, my name's Helene.
I watch you closely, your eyes as grey as doves.
I am a woman. I'm telling you, Levine.

My nipples rise and blush. It's not obscene.
It's been so long since I was touched with love,
though I am nude and faceless, named Helene.

We circle each other but we keep it clean.
I'm hot as a bug on top of a stove.
I am a woman, I'm telling you, Levine,

you could do worse. I lean
on furs, I am a nymph in a grove.
I am nude and faceless. My name's Helene

though I've been drawn in blocks of hair and skin.
Come a little closer, rub
it in. I am a woman. I'm telling you, Levine,

it's a nightmare. I walked in on the wrong scene
and found you. It's hard enough
to be nude and faceless, named Helene,
and still a woman. I'm telling you, Levine.

THE RED SHOES

take me everywhere I'm going, although
sometimes I don't want to get there at
all. They are unwieldy and have a bounce
of their own, which doesn't particularly
suit my personality, but they are sturdy
and will last for years.

Whereas the slippers my mother wears
take her from room to room, and are
smooth as her hands which do nothing,
or turn the pages of my childhood in which
she did not participate.

In the basement of my building, there are boxes
of shoes, discarded although they are new.
They shine in their boxes like eyes, but
are not as fine as my red shoes, which sail
through life as if there were a party every
day, though the parties are essentially life-
less, and nobody there ever walks in a straight line.

FARMERS

Farmers, my mother would say,
need rain. She imagined their raw faces,
the green reflections in their eyes,
the sound in the cornfields.

In the kitchen, my mother carried
her lameness around like a loved pet,
pulled herself to the window.
I sat where I was, my back to my mother,
hoping for weather to come to the only house
left standing on the block,
the polished blue linoleum floor
with nicks in the corners, the dirt
under the carpet in the other room.

My mother waited for farmers
to save her with their red hands,
their pitchforks, waited for them
to walk through the streets, straw
in their hair, a hunger for mother.

Miles away, the farmers listened
for rain, would not have understood
the still air in our house, or mother's eyes
pinned to the window. And I waited
for any stranger to find me hidden
in dark quilts, my suitcases packed
and ready for years. I waited for the weather
to change, waited for something,
knowing nothing of farmers.

WHITE FOX

for Garrett

You were standing in the doorway
waiting for me, wearing white fox.
It looked as if it were part of you,
as if you had given birth.

By *white fox* you mean *beautiful,
a wild and coveted life.* I mean
you were waiting for me and people
walked by, keeping their distance.

They could see your small hands; they
were able to choose. But I knew
I had to walk out the door, recognize you.
There was nowhere else to go.

By *white fox* I mean *dangerous, untouched,*
the dancer nobody knows how to reach
when he stares at a fixed point in space
as if it were a white fox.

IMPERATIVES

Find something old
that is not a religious artifact.
Find something so old its points
are worn, its print illegible.
Find something that will not
tell you the time.

Forget I asked you for anything.
Ask me instead to tell you
one important incident from my past.
Touch the story as if it had no point,
its corners smooth.

Say I am sorry I lost your lucky ring.
Place the ring on the table by the door.
Walk around the table until you know
every facet of the ring's history.
Tell me its story in a language
I can understand.

Speak until the edges of your voice
rub against each other and I can no longer
distinguish sound from shadow.

Take the object you found and destroy it.
The ring on the table has become a clock
that is never wrong. It will tell you:
Come to me tonight.
Wear your best white shirt.

CROSSING THE BLUE BRIDGE

I've been this way before, you say
as we cross the paintbox blue bridge
into Indiana. A sign greets us, predictable
as an almanac: WELCOME TO ROCKPORT. GREEN'S
DRUGSTORE. FIRST BAPTIST CHURCH. SEASON'S
GREETINGS. It is April. Forsythia comes
over us suddenly like a fever. Its yellow
fingers cover the loose and dingy gates
where women gather after services, cutouts
from a storybook in their hats and white hymnbooks.

We never worship. We are together although each time
should have been the last. We try to make conversation,
kill time. We know it will matter later on, when we
look back. What we don't have is courage. What we have
is April hanging over us in Indiana. Season's Greetings.

LETTER FROM ONE PART OF KENTUCKY TO ANOTHER

I am standing at the window, hands
behind my back, the way you would.
You stand, facing away, holding your hands
over the black stove, studying them, turning
them slowly like old papers or photographs.

What I remember most is the small triangle of light
on your hand the last time we made love.
The lights outside, you said, looked like spaceships.
And how cold it was, for Kentucky. How you wanted to
get out. Go home. I couldn't breathe. It was, of course,
the size of the room, the shabbiness. But it was you,
silent, crawling inside me, closing me like a jackknife.

The windows in your house shut down the darkness.
No curtains, no shades. I find myself always standing
in the same position, waiting to grow into your shape,
your size. Waiting to feel your hands, which I know
you study even in your dreams, on my face.

You are inside me. A dry leaf in a child's hand
burns and disintegrates. I am standing at the window
watching a cardinal tremble in the cold winds, red
as the Kentucky sun which is falling away, burning
away as quickly as you, going up in ashes
over the black stove.

THE BURNING WINDOW: VARIATIONS ON A THEME

The elevator stops between floors
but there is no one hungry in the building.

The walls are in fact alive
but have no time for the residents.

In the building's afternoon haze
you would think the building is burning.

A sister speaks to a wife, which explains
the hot yellow color of her burning skin,

the rash of words she cannot contain
until they burn.

In a building across the way, a woman speaks
to the walls and the hot red mouth of the fire

which she knows will love her as she burns.
I live in a room without windows

although the hungry sister burns in the center
of my room. I will keep her, imprison her

warmth, the flickering shapes she makes,
the window she creates in the brick wall.

I live in a room without windows, but
there is a burning window across the way.

No one knows who keeps the constant fire going
but I can guess.

THE OCCUPANT

The occupant is as able-bodied
as you and I. He remains in his chair
because he wants to. The room is well-
lit and well-ventilated. The occupant
chooses the darkness. A woman standing
in the doorway understands the silence
she hears and loves it like a sister.

The threads of his nightmare lie
in the palm of his hand. He builds
a house around the interior of his
room. The very special images at the
back of his eyes gather in corners,
pronounce syllables he hears in his
sleep with care. Soon he will not sleep.
He will not separate night from day.
He will perhaps become an artist and multiply.

THE RED STAIRWAY

After the painting by Ben Shahn

I

Beyond the red stairway, anyone would be waiting.
But our man is missing more than a face,
a reputation. He can barely navigate the ground
he has to cover, yet he climbs the stairs hour
after hour, has another hat at home,
a leg that buckled under him like love.

A friend gave himself to the sea
like a bundle of old clothes, but this man
has money hidden in his mattress, a promise
from a woman he has committed to memory.
He will not die, not without witnesses.
Somewhere, a painter mixes the color of death,
which is not red.

II

She will wait for him by the sea. It will
take him years to reach her, but she will never age.
Red is her color. He dreams of her in red
or of wounds that heal in the shape of the moon
or footprints on the beach.

There is no moon now, only the shape
of a man carrying a basket, which is the moon
turned inside out, its guts strung like fruit
over the landscape.

She will wait for him to turn at the top,
look backward at the others along the shore.
Their light falls around him, but he will not notice,
will not watch the spine of the ocean
rise like a hurt animal.

THE SLIDE

The best in life is close to the ground,
especially the pain I feel
when I hit bottom. But I can start all over again,
any time. Climb the ladder, catch my breath.
Although I'm getting a little old
for this trick, I won't stop. I wait
until sunset when the children go home.
Then, the light sits easy on the steel.
Even the dead leaves shine.

I know you have to keep busy,
but I need time for myself. It's impossible
to get you outside in the air.
You stay miles away from my house
although I would never invite you.
You are afraid of the children
although they are harmless.

The say I'm afraid of heights
but that's just part of my act.
I want to land. I love the icy steel
beneath me, the hands of the earth
on my thighs. You're too busy drinking wine
and looking out windows. You won't even watch.
You won't even pick me up when I break.

CHEMO-POET

CHEMO-POET

I look in the mirror. "Hello, Chemo-Poet." I am bald and
missing my left breast. I have a clean scar and can feel the
bone and my heart beneath my fingers. I feel the lost breast
living, pulsing in a jar somewhere, a pathologist's jar,
waiting for morning, waiting to find itself home again. Hello,
Chemo-Poet, how long have you got? Most people don't
know how long they've got either, but they don't have
documents written on their bodies to remind them.

I go outside, always in disguise. I have a wig that makes me
look like Mary Tyler Moore, but not me, never me. So I won't
wear it. Instead, I wear a scarf and wrap it around me, its
vibrant colors screaming "Gypsy, gypsy." I wear makeup to
cover the absences of blood the drugs cause. The not-me is
beautiful, my friends say, a radiance of color and disguise, a
Mardi Gras of hope and death, a doll with missing pieces.

I LAND AT THE MASH UNIT
IN THE TWILIGHT ZONE

"What's this," Hawkeye hisses. "It's a woman. Trauma to the chest," mourns B.J. The wound gapes before him, the grinning mouth of a cave, the sharp door to a nightmare. It's too much, too much, he thinks as all the king's horses and all the king's men tumble before his eyes. "Enough." Margaret "Hotlips" Houlihan oozes over, blond and clear, a bell in the darkened room. She wants to donate part of herself, give her own flesh over to that vast, broken place on the table. "Yes, yes, of course we can . . . "

Music

A voice intrudes: "You think you are at a MASH unit, a place where doctors and nurses give you a chance in their own dreams—where with a simple snap of a knife you will get put together again. Actually you are . . . "

THE GENERIC ONCOLOGIST

"Why are you here?" is the first question he asks me. Why am I here? Over his desk, facing his patients, are photographs of his entire family: wife, children, even a dog. Why are they there? Are they there to reassure me that there are families, that I might get one? Are they there to reassure him that he won't catch my sadness, my fear? Are they a Greek chorus saying, "Cancer, cancer. Step up and say the word that explains why you are here."

But I know better, and I do not want to say the word that changes life into something else. I sit on my uncomfortable chair, flanked by two good friends, and say it: "I am here for chemotherapy." And the wife and the children and the dog look on at the doctor and me. "Are there any questions?" he asks after giving me heart-stopping statistics. This is serious business, the statistics say.

I am speechless for the first time I can remember. My friends ask articulate questions, notebooks in hand. I am told I will remember little of this interview. I inch into my body and a world where none of this is happening. I hear little, say little, but my friends write everything down. "How long do I have?" I ask silently, not wanting to know. I hear him say, "You are going to lose your hair." I say, "I lost my breast, now I am going to lose my hair." "Your hair grows back," he says.

I GO TO THE WIG LADY

The wig lady is fuzzy, almost not there at all. It is as if all the winds got together and tried to manufacture a woman, but something went wrong, and little bits and pieces keep getting away and flying all over the place. I go to see her because within weeks I will be completely bald.

I find my way to her by going up several flights of stairs and through winding black and white tiled hallways. Her office is cluttered, colorless. She, too, is colorless. We are surrounded by dozens of bodiless, painted heads, all wearing seasons and centuries of real, 100% human hair. The heads have no voices, and it is just as well, for the wig lady doesn't like to talk. She doesn't ask my name or how I am. She does produce this live, squirming black mass which I recognize at once as mine. In a moment of rage and fear, I name it "Kitty" and know that it alone will hide my shameful secret and allow me to move among the living.

I sit in the mirror in my perfectly constructed basic black dress and my sterling silver earrings and my expensive makeup. "Not bad for forty," I say.

"You're a plain Jane," she says, "a plain Jane. But you manage to look attractive."

MY WORLD

I know the dizzying path from my bed to the bathroom, the icy feel of the sink under my fingers, my chin. The smell of the bath oils and powders on the shelf. I know exactly how many minutes it will take Martha to run down the hill to my house when I call her for help. I know by heart the stained-glass colors of my night light that I leave on every night although I can now find my way through the house blind. I know the hard, white edges of my wicker chair where I first felt my hair prickle and then die. I know that outside, mysteriously, people are always finding something to celebrate. Thanksgiving, Christmas, New Year's. Lights, gift wraps. The crinkle of ribbons. A friend gets married. Another has a baby.

Here, in my world, I know only the silk of my cat against my skin, always there in my bed, always there when I'm ill. I breathe a cat's breath, rumble in my chest—a purr. I want to slink into a cat's sleep, leave my body for awhile, the smell of medicine in my body, my rooms, the white foam I vomit. But every time I look, it's midnight. I take my "rescue" pill. I sit in the wicker chair. I expect to hear the sound of the devil clanging through the hallway outside my door.

DRACULA MEETS A CHEMO-POET

Dracula comes through my window, hungry as usual. Fine, I say, hungry too, hungry for the kiss, the bite, everlasting life. He shows up in his rented suit and fine white shirt. He is wearing his company manners. "Would you be so kind," he says. "Yes." And I picture his wings protecting me in the dark skies. Dracula drinks my blood and vomits six hours later. In three weeks he loses all his hair.

I DREAM

I am a male convict about to be killed by lethal injection.
Somehow they zapped me while I was in the bathroom but it
didn't work. I run out into a room full of reporters and
strangers and scream, "Listen to me. I can tell you all about
drugs. I know all about drugs."

I am on a bus and a handicapped person gets on. I get dirty
looks from the passengers because I don't stand up to let
him sit. "Don't you know what happened to me!" I scream.
"Look!" I pull off my scarf and unbutton my shirt. "How dare
you! How dare you think I am like you!"

I confront my mother, who just found out. "Look, look," I
cry. I pull off my scarf and unbutton my shirt. "That's
nothing," she says. "That's nothing."

I VISIT THE PROSTHESIS LADY

She is cold and gray and properly dressed, buttoned right up to her chin in a crisp blue shirt and sensible shoes. She stands like a soldier and stares at me. Instantly I know I've been a bad girl. Somehow I've gone and lost a breast or given myself cancer; and worse, far worse, I haven't been wearing my wonderful, human-like prosthesis, although no one has told me I must.

She stands me in front of a mirror and points out that my right shoulder is lower than my left, strong evidence that my body has been missing the weight of a left breast. How much can it weigh, I ask myself, having always been an A minus or less. Couldn't it be the thirty pounds of books I carry? I ask. I'm bad. Not only am I off-balance but I ask questions too. She marches out one prosthesis after another but none fit. I keep stuffing them in my bra and they are cold and warm at the same time, sweet and squishy; and I want to sail them across the room and drop them out the window on the heads of women who have hair and breasts. Finally, inevitably, we find a fit. Size zero. I am a zero. It was meant to be.

I'm a zero and I'm bad. I'm getting worse. I tell her I don't really need the box it comes in. "Yes, yes; it will lose its shape if you don't use it. You must put it to bed at night after carefully washing and rinsing and drying it." "The care and feeding," she says. My baby. Which will never grow, ask questions. Which will never die. "You need pockets in your bras," she tells me. "Can't I make do without them?" "What if one falls out and lands on the floor?" she asks.

I always think on my feet. Little squishy baby falls on the floor in the middle of my teaching a class. "Silly putty," I will say. "I never have been able to kick the habit." I give in, have pockets made—pink and lavender and black buntings for my baby girl. I picture the prosthesis lady in heaven with the wig lady, both serene in the knowledge that they have set bad girls straight.

THE PRINCE

The Prince rides by all the houses in the neighborhood,
strong and luminous, completely, delightfully whole. His
hair flows in the wind and he is as one with his black horse.
Their sweat mingles, their breath sings in the low winds.
The prince carries a glass breast on a velvet pillow—the
perfect fit. Just the right size.

Yet the prince flies right by my house, never stopping, never
even looking in my window. I wait. The voices of my sisters
howl in the darkness.

HERE AND THERE

I go in and out of fantasy. I don't much like it *here,* and *there,* there is at least the possibility of magic. When you are good, you are rewarded, and the idea of bad is not the same as it is here. There, you can think evil thoughts about your mother, eat butter and meat and sour cream, and you will not get punished, not get cancer.

There, you can say the right word or the right group of words and you will kill the wicked witch and get her house and her car and all her riches. There, you may meet a kindhearted dove or rabbit or old woman and get led through a secret door where someone will grant all your wishes.

Not like here. Here, they cart away parts of your body piece by piece and your hair and your eyelashes fall out and you collect them in a plastic bag and put them in a drawer so that you will always remember. No one will take them away and say prayers over them or make magic so that you will become whole again. Here, no one forgives you, and you cannot forgive yourself.

HEALING BY COMPUTER

My brother has reached THE LORD on his computer terminal
screen and THE HOUSE OF THE LORD, white on black, and
he searches and the messages flip up on the screen and there
it is: THE FOUR SIGNS OF BIRTH and THE MARK OF THE
CROSS and soon we will go into another room, sunlit and
bare, for the healing.

Nowhere in the house is a book that is not on white magic or
the teachings of Zen and the only picture on the wall is
Christ and I am forced to sleep on pillows filled with
pebbles and a mattress as hard as life.

As much as I thought I hated it, I miss my house which is
filled with cat fur and clothes hanging from the walls and the
bed posts and books falling from their shelves and my bed, a
harvest of flowers.

But I close my eyes and can almost get back there again
during the click of his fingers on the keys and the feel of his
hot, healing hands on my back which is hard and tight and
unforgiving.

THE BODY IS NOT CONSTANT

"The body is not constant," the woman on the telephone says, meaning *sports,* meaning you cannot always have the perfect score, perfect form on the tennis court, in the gym. The dancer practices for hours in front of the mirror; the actress loses the white line on the stage. Meaning *perfection,* meaning *illusion,* meaning *business.* "The body is not constant," she says, her voice thinning.

So that is why my back has somehow moved to my chest, and my left breasts jumps when I move my right arm. So that is why someone else stares at me in the window of the subway car, and I cannot hear the wrong words coming at me anymore, and that is why I can only see out of my third eye.

I DON'T

Come on, they say, why not? But I edge toward the other end, never the center—or away. Shadowy night store windows, or a quick thief on mute carpets at let's say one of the best stores. But quicker than the blink and I'm gone. I don't even see whole, only a sudden shock of arm or ear at once, and even that blind, squint, or prayer. Never in full light, even at home, and never hairshine to toe for anyone's sake.

Funny thing happened to me on the way to my body. They kept taking pieces away, one by one, until "Scarbody," he said, and I can't look in the mirror anymore, all of me all at the same time.

THE BLUES

THE BLUES: The Great Woods Blues Festival, 1987

"I'll never get out of these blues alive."
—John Lee Hooker

The Difference between Reality and Media I

If this were the movies, he'd be back,
drawing slowly on his pipe, listening
to your demands. You are willing to turn
yourself over and over like an embryo
in a science film, your own voice silenced.
But love backfires, and you find yourself
listening to live blues, which is where you belong.
The audience pitched forward, music falling thick
through the trees, blues men jumping on the stage.
And although the names and faces change, the rap
is always the same: "Hello, Boston! Are you ready?
Ready to boogie?"

Backstage

Suddenly you can't remember your childhood, know
you didn't come from Chicago or Mississippi.
All you can think of is going backstage and meeting
John Lee Hooker, but you don't have a ticket
and nobody's asking and that's the story
of your life. Somehow you get there. In the dimness
of faces and cigarette smoke you ask yourself
why old blues men always wear suits and hats
even in the hottest weather, and what do you say
to someone like that, over seventy and a myth.
Hooker kisses your hand.

The Nighthawks

You remember the painting. This is the music.
Here, no catatonic eye turned inward, no examination
of body and soul. They play, all dressed up in light.
You forget you have been standing up all day and
nobody's waiting at home with a cup of coffee.
This isn't baseball or ballet, and if you tried
to explain it, nobody would know what you were talking
about.

The Difference between Reality and Media II

You want it to go on like a book, encounters
and retreats folding into each other
with no end in sight. The dialogue of lovers—
her inevitable song, her return as she clicks
upstairs shifting a bundle of greens, wearing
her high heeled shoes. The picture of love
and health. But she's gone and it's some old man
instead, asking for charity, blues running down
his cheeks. Stacks of newspapers fade.
Somebody's story lies open.

You Think of the Blues as a Place:

where you always have a free ticket
which is in utter darkness
which is restless as a cat
which has its secrets like anyplace else
which has marks all over its body
which welcomes people like you